Sanjeev Kapoor's
Pressure Cooking

Sanjeev Kapoor's

Pressure Cooking

In association with Alyona Kapoor

Popular
Prakashan

www.popularprakashan.com

POPULAR PRAKASHAN PVT. LTD.
301, Mahalaxmi Chambers
22, Bhulabhai Desai Road
Mumbai - 400026

© 2008 Sanjeev Kapoor
First Published 2008
First Reprint April 2008
Second Reprint March 2009

(4107)
ISBN: 978-81-7991-359-8

Photography: Bharat Bhirangi

PRINTED IN INDIA
by Vikalp Binding Pvt. Ltd.
C-62/4, Okhla, Phase II
Delhi-110020

Published by Ramdas Bhatkal
for Popular Prakashan Pvt. Ltd.
301, Mahalaxmi Chambers
22, Bhulabhai Desai Road
Mumbai - 400026

AUTHOR'S NOTE

Today, when homemakers are also breadwinners, a pressure cooker is one of the most essential of kitchen appliances. Few homes can do without this time and energy-saving device which helps to produce a meal in a matter of minutes. Gone are the days when foods were left to simmer for hours over a low heat to the desired perfection. With a pressure cooker, a quick boil, a lid securely fastened and a few hisses later, a complete meal can be served with the minimum fuss and waste of time.

For those who have not yet discovered the joys of pressure-cooking, here's why you should get one right away and make your time in the kitchen both enjoyable and less stressful:

- Food cooks faster in a pressure cooker thus saving time.
- Because food cooks faster less fuel is used resulting in a saving of gas, electricity or other fuels.
- Food is cooked under pressure at a higher boiling point than water, resulting in the food being rendered more bacteria and germ free.
- The nutrient levels of food are preserved as food is cooked for a shorter time.

- Many food can be cooked at the same time in a pressure cooker resulting in savings of time and fuel.

While pressure-cooking has many advantages, it is important to use the cooker safely and wisely for optimum benefits. Here are some tips to get the most out of your cooker:

Safety

- Read the manufacturer's instructions carefully for safe and economic use of the pressure cooker.
- Always check that the vent or safety valve and weights are clean and in good condition before using the pressure cooker. Ensure that the rubber gasket is flexible and clean.
- Never use less than the minimum amount of liquid as recommended by the manufacturer.
- Do not fill the cooker more than two-thirds full while cooking most foods or the half full when cooking foods which expand on cooking or are made up of a lot of liquid, like dals, soups etc.
- Do not use more than a quarter cup of oil or fat while cooking in a pressure cooker.

- Bring the food to a boil on high heat before sealing the cooker with a lid. Continue cooking over a high heat till full pressure is reached and then lower the heat to maintain the pressure.
- Always check to make sure the pressure has dropped back to normal before opening the locking lid on a pressure cooker.
- When in a hurry, you can release the pressure by running cold water over the lid. Make sure that you do not run the water over the vent or valve.

Cooking

- Follow the cooking times as given in the recipes. Cooking for a longer or less time will affect the texture and the tenderness of the food.
- Trim the fat from meat, and cut meat, poultry, fish and vegetables into uniform pieces to ensure even cooking.
- When cooking different foods together, cut those that cook more quickly into larger pieces and those that cook more slowly into smaller pieces for even cooking.
- Do not fill the cooker too much - the more food in the pressure cooker, the longer it will take to reach full pressure.
- Thick sauces, gravies or fats should not be counted as part of the minimum liquid necessary for the cooker.

- As salt raises the boiling point of water and delays pressurization, add salt at the end of pressure cooking.
- While steaming foods in an aluminum pressure cooker, add one teaspoon of vinegar or lemon skins to the water to help prevent stains or discolouration.

I have included a number of recipes for every course in a meal from soup to dessert. As you will see all foods can be cooked in a pressure cooker with no difference to taste or texture. As always, every recipe has been tried and tested and serves four persons.

So take the pressure out of cooking by using a pressure cooker for tasty, nutritious meals in a fraction of the time!

Happy Cooking!

Acknowledgements

Afsheen Panjwani
Anand Bhandiwad
Anil Bhandari
Anupa Das
Ashwini Patwardhan
Bharati Anand
Bhartendu Sharma
Drs. Meena and Ram Prabhoo
Gajendra Mule
Ganesh Pednekar
Harpal Singh Sokhi
Jayadeep Chaubal
Jyotsna and Mayur Dvivedi
Kalpana Deshmukh
Lohana Khaandaan
Mahendra Ghanekar

Mrs. Lata Lohana and
Capt. K. K. Lohana
N. K. Krishnanand
Namrata and Sanjiv Bahl
Neelima Acharya
Neena Murdeshwar
Pooja and Rajeev Kapoor
Rajeev Matta
Rita D'Souza
Rutika Samtani
Saurabh Mishra
Smeeta Bhatkal
Tripta Bhagattjee
Trupti Kale
Vinayak Gawande

CONTENTS

Soups, Snacks and Starters

Red Pumpkin Soup   13

Tomato Soup   16

Mixed Vegetable Soup   18

Handvo   20

Patra   24

Sandwich Dhokla   26

Caramel Popcorn   29

Vegetable Idli   30

Main Course - Vegetarian

Tomato with Penne   33

Rajma Rasmisa   34

Sai Bhaji   36

Soya Granule Sabzi   39

Nadur Palak   41

Methi Baingan   42

Rishi Panchami Sabzi   45

Pumpkin Curry   46

Vegetable Stew   48

Bharli Vangi   51

Main Course - Non-Vegetarian

Dal Gosht   53

Bhatinda Mutton Curry   56

Steamed Tandoor Pomfret   58

Malvani Mutton   59

Kolhapuri Chicken   61

Dahi Ka Gosht	65		Gehu Ki Khichdi	90
Chicken Cafreal	67		Herbed Rice With Mushrooms	92
Bhuna Kukda	69		Chicken Pulao	94
Methi Chicken	72		Vegetable Biryani	96
Masala Prawns	74			

Dals and Cereals

Langar Ki Dal	76			
Shahi Prawn Pulao	78			
Chane Jaiselmer Ke	80			
Mutton Khichda	82			
Brown Rice Vegetable Pilaf	84			
Suran Ki Khichdi	86			
Palakwali Dal	88			

Desserts

Chocolate Modak	98
Gajar Halwa	100
Dudhi Halwa	101
Kharvas	102

RED PUMPKIN SOUP

1 kilogram red pumpkin (*lal bhopla/kaddu*), diced

4 tablespoons butter

3 bay leaves

15-20 black peppercorns

3 large onions, sliced

4 cups Vegetable Stock (see below) or water

salt to taste

1 teaspoon white pepper powder

1 tablespoon lemon juice

½ cup fresh cream (*malai*)

- Heat the butter in a pressure cooker; add the bay leaves and peppercorns. Add the onions and sauté for two minutes.

- Add the diced pumpkin and sauté for half a minute. Add four cups of water and cook under pressure until pressure is released once (one whistle).

- Strain and reserve the stock. Purée the vegetables.

- Add the reserved stock and one cup of water to the purée.

- Add the salt and white pepper powder and bring to a boil. Stir in the lemon juice.

- Serve hot, garnished with fresh cream.

Note : *This soup can be served in the shells of scooped out small red pumpkins, no bigger than the size of a coconut.*

Vegetable Stock

Place 1 sliced onion, 1 sliced carrot, a 2-3 inch celery stalk, 2 garlic cloves, 1 bay leaf, 5-6 black peppercons and 2-3 cloves in a pan with 5 cups of water and bring to a boil. Simmer for fifteen minutes and strain. Cool and store in a refrigerator. Vegetable stock will keep for two to three days in a refrigerator.

TOMATO SOUP

10-12 medium tomatoes, quartered
2 slices bread, cut into cubes
1 teaspoon sugar
¼ cup cream
½ tablespoon oil
1 tablespoon butter
1 bay leaf

8-10 black peppercorns
1 medium onion, sliced
4 garlic cloves, chopped
2-inch celery stalk, chopped
½ medium carrot, sliced
salt to taste
1 tablespoon chopped fresh parsley

- Toast the bread cubes in an oven or frying pan to make croutons.

- Mix together the sugar and cream.

- Heat the oil and butter in a pressure cooker; add the bay leaf, four or five peppercorns and the onion and sauté until translucent. Add the garlic and celery and sauté for a few seconds.

- Add the carrot, tomatoes and salt. Sauté for one minute and add three cups of water. Seal the cooker with the lid and cook over medium heat till the pressure is released four or five times (four or five whistles).

- Remove the lid when the pressure has reduced completely and strain. Reserve the liquid. Remove the peppercorns and bay leaf and discard. Leave the rest of the solids to cool. Purée in a blender till smooth. Pass the purée through a sieve or strainer.

- Add the reserved liquid to the puréed tomatoes and adjust the consistency. Place back on heat.

- Add the salt, and the remaining peppercorns and simmer for a couple of minutes.

- Just before serving, stir in the cream and sugar mixture. Serve hot, garnished with parsley and toasted croutons.

Soups, Snacks and Starters

MIXED VEGETABLE SOUP

1 medium onion, chopped

1 medium potato, chopped

1 medium carrot, chopped

6-8 fresh button mushrooms, chopped

¼ medium cabbage, chopped

6-8 French beans, chopped

4-5 small cauliflower florets, grated

1 medium green capsicum, chopped

1 tablespoon oil

2 bay leaves

2 teaspoons wholewheat flour (*atta*)

salt to taste

white pepper powder to taste

3 cups Vegetable Stock (page 14)

2 cups skimmed milk

- Heat the oil in a pressure cooker; add the bay leaves and onion and sauté for two minutes over medium heat. Add the potato, carrot, mushrooms, cabbage, French beans and cauliflower. Stir and cook over high heat for three or four minutes.

- Sprinkle the wholewheat flour and cook, stirring continuously, over medium heat, (for two minutes). Add the salt and white pepper powder.

- Stir in the vegetable stock and bring to a boil. Add the capsicum.
- Seal the cooker with the lid and cook over medium heat till the pressure is released twice (two whistles).
- Remove the lid when the pressure has reduced completely and gradually stir in the skimmed milk. Simmer for three or four minutes.
- Remove the bay leaves, adjust seasoning and serve piping hot.

HANDVO

1 cup rice
½ cup split pigeon peas
(*arhar dal/toovar dal*)
¼ cup split green gram
(*dhuli moong dal*)
2 tablespoons split Bengal gram
(*chana dal*)
2 tablespoons split black gram
(*dhuli urad dal*)
½ cup sour yogurt
2 teaspoons soda bicarbonate
salt to taste
4 teaspoons sugar

2 teaspoons red chilli powder
½ teaspoon turmeric powder
1 medium carrot, grated
½ cup shelled green peas, boiled
5 tablespoons oil
2 dried red chillies
2 cloves
1 bay leaf
a pinch of asafoetida (*hing*)
2 teaspoons mustard seeds
1 tablespoon lemon juice
3 tablespoons toasted sesame seeds
(*til*)

- Soak the rice with all the *dals* in five cups of water for two hours. Drain. Grind the rice to a coarse paste and add enough water to make a batter of medium thick consistency. Mix in the yogurt and one teaspoon of soda bicarbonate. Cover the batter and leave to stand in a dark place for two or three hours to ferment.

- Stir in the salt, sugar, chilli powder and turmeric powder into the batter. Mix in the grated carrot and green peas.

- Heat the oil in a pan; add the red chillies, cloves, bay leaf, asafoetida and mustard seeds and sauté till the seeds begin to splutter.

- Sprinkle the remaining soda bicarbonate over the batter and stir the lemon juice into it. Immediately pour the hot spices into the batter and whisk briskly.

- Grease a ring mould. Pour the batter into it till half full. Sprinkle the toasted sesame seeds generously over the top.

- Place about two kilograms of clean sand in a large pressure cooker. Place the ring mould in the sand carefully, pressing down till it is embedded about half way into the sand. Cover the cooker with the lid but without the gasket and whistle.

- Place over high heat for ten minutes. Lower heat to medium and cook the *handvo* till a skewer inserted into it comes out clean. It may take forty to forty-five minutes.

- Cool slightly and unmould the *handvo*. Cut into thick slices and serve hot with Green Chutney.

Green Chutney

Grind together 1 cup fresh coriander leaves, ½ cup fresh mint leaves, 2-3 green chillies, black salt to taste, ¼ cup sugar and 1 tablespoon lemon juice to a smooth paste using a little water if required.

PATRA

12 colocassia leaves (*arbi patta*)

1½ cups gram flour (*besan*)

2 teaspoons coriander powder

1 teaspoon cumin powder

1 teaspoon red chilli powder

1 teaspoon turmeric powder

2 teaspoons sesame seeds (*til*)

salt to taste

1 teaspoon green chilli paste

1 teaspoon ginger paste

4 tablespoons oil

2 tablespoons tamarind pulp

3½ tablespoons grated jaggery

1 teaspoon mustard seeds

a pinch of asafoetida (*hing*)

¼ cup grated fresh coconut

4 tablespoons chopped fresh coriander leaves

- Remove the thick stems from the leaves. Wash the leaves, wipe dry and set aside.

- Mix together the gram flour, coriander powder, cumin powder, chilli powder and turmeric powder in a bowl. Add the sesame seeds, salt, green chilli paste, ginger paste and two tablespoons of oil and mix well.

Pressure Cooking

- Mix together the tamarind pulp and jaggery and mix into the gram flour mixture.

- Place a leaf, shiny side face down, on a work surface. Spread the paste evenly over the back of the leaf. Place another leaf over it, but with its tapering end in the opposite direction of the first one. Spread some paste over it. Fold in the four edges and gently roll into a tight cylinder. Do the same with the rest of the leaves and paste. Place the cylinders on a perforated plate or a sieve.

- Heat some water in a pressure cooker and place a metal ring or trivet in it. Place the sieve on the ring and seal the cooker with the lid. Steam without the weight for about twenty-five to thirty minutes, or till cooked. Insert a thin knife into the *patra* to check for doneness. If the knife comes out clean, the *patra* is cooked. Remove the *patra* and leave to cool. Cut into ¼-inch thick slices.

- Heat the remaining oil in a *kadai*; add the mustard seeds. When they begin to splutter, add the asafoetida and the slices of *patra*. Sauté till golden brown. Serve hot, garnished with coconut and coriander leaves.

Soups, Snacks and Starters

SANDWICH DHOKLA

1 cup rice

¼ cup split black gram (*dhuli urad dal*)

¼ cup skimmed milk sour yogurt

salt to taste

2 teaspoons ginger paste

1 ½ teaspoons green chilli paste

½ teaspoon soda bicarbonate

1 tablespoon lemon juice

½ cup thick Green Chutney (page 23)

2 tablespoons chopped fresh coriander leaves

- Dry-roast the rice and the *dal* over medium heat for four or five minutes. Cool and grind into a moderately coarse powder.

- Put the powder into a bowl. Add the yogurt and-one-and-a-half cups of warm water. Mix thoroughly to make a smooth batter of pouring consistency. Stir in the salt.

- Leave the batter to ferment for eight to ten hours. Add the ginger paste and green chilli paste to the batter and mix well.

Pressure Cooking

- Bring some water to a boil in a pressure cooker.

- Pour half the batter in a separate bowl. In a small bowl mix one-fourth teaspoon of soda bicarbonate and half a tablespoon of lemon juice. Add to the batter and whisk well. Repeat this procedure for the remaining batter just before putting it into the steamer.

- Pour the batter into a *thali* and place it in the pressure cooker. Steam without the weight for eight to ten minutes. Test for doneness with a knife. If the knife comes out clean, it is cooked. Remove from the cooker and spread green chutney over the *dhokla* while hot.

- Pour the remaining batter over the chutney and steam again for ten minutes. Remove from the cooker, cool slightly, and garnish with coriander leaves. Cut into desired shapes and serve hot.

CARAMEL POPCORN

²/₃ cup dried corn kernels   4 tablespoons brown sugar

- Heat a pressure cooker. Add the corn kernels and cover with the inverted lid.
- Shake the cooker from time to time. As the corn begins to pop, quickly sprinkle brown sugar and replace the lid.
- Continue shaking the cooker from time to time. Uncover as soon as the popping stops and transfer the popcorn to a bowl.
- Stir when slightly cooled and serve.

VEGETABLE IDLI

1 cup parboiled rice (*ukda chawal*)

½ cup split black gram (*dhuli urad dal*)

salt to taste

1 medium carrot, grated

4-5 French beans, chopped

2-3 cauliflower florets, grated

½ medium green capsicum, chopped

1 inch ginger

2 tablespoons oil

15-20 black peppercorns, crushed

2 tablespoons chopped fresh coriander leaves

- Soak the rice and *urad dal* separately for at least four hours. Drain and grind the rice with some water to a coarse batter; grind the *dal* with water to a thin batter.

- Mix both the batters together, adding water if necessary, to make a batter of dropping consistency.

- Add the salt, cover and leave to ferment overnight or for four or five hours, in a warm place.

Pressure Cooking

- Add the vegetables to the fermented batter and mix well.

- Lightly grease the *idli* moulds with oil. Pour a spoonful of batter into each mould. Sprinkle each *idli* with crushed peppercorns and chopped coriander leaves.

- Heat some water in a pressure cooker and place the *idli* stand in it. Seal the cooker with the lid and steam without the weight for ten minutes, or till done.

- Serve hot with chutney.

TOMATO WITH PENNE

250 grams penne
(quill-shaped pasta)
1 cup tomato purée
3½ tablespoons olive oil
2 medium onions, sliced
6 garlic cloves, crushed
1 teaspoon red chilli flakes

1 teaspoon dried oregano
5-6 fresh basil leaves, roughly torn
salt to taste
1 teaspoon sugar
2 tablespoons grated Parmesan
cheese

- Heat the olive oil in a pressure cooker; add the onion and garlic and sauté till light brown. Add the chilli flakes, dried oregano and basil and sauté for one minute.
- Add the penne and sauté for half a minute. Add the tomato purée, salt, sugar and two cups of water. Seal the cooker with the lid and cook over medium heat till the pressure is released twice (two whistles). Remove the lid when the pressure has reduced completely and transfer the penne to a bowl. Serve hot, garnished with Parmesan cheese.

Main Course - Vegetarian

RAJMA RASMISA

1½ cups red kidney beans (*rajma*),
soaked overnight

3 tablespoons oil

2 bay leaves

2 medium onions, chopped

1 inch ginger, chopped

6-8 garlic cloves, chopped

2 teaspoons red chilli powder

1 tablespoon coriander powder

½ teaspoon turmeric powder

1 teaspoon cumin powder

3 medium tomatoes, chopped

salt to taste

1 teaspoon *garam masala* powder

1 tablespoon chopped fresh
coriander leaves

- Cook the *rajma* with five cups of water under pressure till the pressure is released five times (five whistles), or completely cooked and soft.

- Heat the oil in a deep pan; add the bay leaves and onions and sauté till golden brown.

- Add the ginger and garlic and continue to sauté for one minute.

Pressure Cooking

- Add the chilli powder, coriander powder, turmeric powder and cumin powder and sauté for a while. Add the tomatoes and salt and cook till soft and pulpy and the oil separates.

- Add the *rajma* with the cooking liquid and mix well. Cook over low heat for fifteen minutes, stirring occasionally. Add the *garam masala* powder and cook for five minutes.

- Garnish with coriander leaves and serve hot with steamed rice.

SAI BHAJI

2 medium bunches (400 grams) spinach

½ medium bunch *khatta* leaves

4 tablespoons oil

½ teaspoon cumin seeds

2 medium onions, finely chopped

1 inch ginger, finely chopped

3-4 green chillies, finely chopped

2 small long brinjals, cut into 1-inch cubes

2 medium potatoes, peeled and cut into 1-inch cubes

4 tablespoons split Bengal gram (*chana dal*), soaked

2 large tomatoes, roughly chopped

¼ teaspoon turmeric powder

1 teaspoon red chilli powder

salt to taste

- Cut the spinach and half the *khatta* leaves into fine shreds.

- Heat the oil in a pressure cooker and add the cumin seeds. When they begin to change colour, add the onions and sauté till golden brown.

- Add the ginger and green chillies and sauté for a few seconds. Add a little water, if required.

- Add the spinach, whole *khatta* leaves, shredded *khatta* leaves, brinjal and potato cubes, soaked *chana dal*, tomatoes, turmeric powder, chilli powder and salt. Stir in two cups of water.

- Seal the cooker with the lid and cook on high heat till the pressure is released once (one whistle). Lower heat and cook for eight to ten minutes longer. Remove the lid when the pressure is released completely.

- Remove the potato cubes with a slotted spoon and blend the remaining mixture with a hand blender. Add the potato cubes. Serve hot.

Pressure Cooking

SOYA GRANULE SABZI

200 grams soya granules
2 medium potatoes, peeled and cut into ½-inch cubes
1 inch ginger
2 green chillies
1 tablespoon oil
1 teaspoon cumin seeds
3 medium onions, chopped

3 medium tomatoes, chopped
1 teaspoon red chilli powder
½ teaspoon turmeric powder
salt to taste
½ cup yogurt
2 tablespoons chopped fresh coriander leaves

- Grind the ginger and green chillies to a fine paste.

- Heat the oil in a pressure cooker; add the cumin seeds. When they begin to change colour, add the onions and sauté till golden brown. Add the ginger-green chilli paste and sauté for half a minute.

Main Course - Vegetarian

- Add the tomatoes and sauté for four or five minutes. Add the chilli powder and turmeric powder and sauté till the oil separates.

- Add the soya granules, potatoes, salt, half a cup of water and yogurt and mix well. Seal the cooker with the lid and cook over medium heat till pressure is released once (one whistle). Remove the lid when the pressure has reduced completely and simmer till almost dry.

- Serve hot, garnished with coriander leaves.

40

NADUR PALAK

250 grams lotus root (*nadur/bhen*)

2 bunches (400 grams) fresh spinach leaves (*palak*), chopped

¼ teaspoon asafoetida (*hing*)

5 tablespoons oil

salt to taste

1 teaspoon red chilli powder

½ teaspoon turmeric powder

1 teaspoon dried ginger powder (*soonth*)

½ teaspoon *garam masala* powder

- Scrape the lotus root well. Cut into thick round slices and wash thoroughly. Mix the asafoetida with one tablespoon of water.

- Heat the oil in a pressure cooker and stir-fry the lotus roots for five minutes. Add the asafoetida mixture, salt and spinach. Add half a cup of water, seal the cooker with the lid and cook over medium heat till the pressure is released three times (three whistles).

- Remove the lid when the pressure has reduced completely. Stir in the chilli powder, turmeric powder and dried ginger powder. Simmer till almost all the water has dried up. Sprinkle *garam masala* powder and serve hot.

Main Course - Vegetarian

METHI BAINGAN

2 bunches (500 grams) fresh
fenugreek leaves *(methi)*, chopped
10-12 small brinjals
salt to taste
2 teaspoons red chilli powder
½ teaspoon dried mango powder
(*amchur*)
2 tablespoons oil
½ teaspoon mustard seeds
8-10 curry leaves
1 green chilli, chopped

2 medium onions, chopped
1½ tablespoons ginger-garlic paste
2 medium tomatoes, chopped
1 teaspoon cumin powder
1 teaspoon coriander powder
½ teaspoon turmeric powder
½ teaspoon *garam masala* powder
2 tablespoons chopped fresh
coriander leaves

- Slit the brinjals lengthways into four keeping the stem intact.
- Rub salt, one teaspoon of chilli powder and the *amchur* into the slit brinjals and set aside.

Pressure Cooking

- Heat the oil in a pressure cooker; add the mustard seeds. When they begin to splutter, add the curry leaves, green chilli and onions and sauté till the onions turn golden.

- Add the ginger-garlic paste and continue to sauté for one minute. Stir in the tomatoes remaining chilli powder, cumin powder and coriander powder. Add the turmeric powder, *garam masala* powder and half a cup of water and bring the mixture to a boil.

- Add the brinjals, fenugreek leaves and salt. Seal the cooker with the lid and cook till the pressure is released once (one whistle). Lower heat and cook for two minutes.

- Take the cooker off the heat and remove the lid when the pressure has reduced. Garnish with coriander leaves and serve hot.

44

RISHI PANCHAMI SABZI

1 medium ridge gourd (*turai*), seeded and cut into 1-inch cubes

2 medium cucumbers, seeded and cut into 1-inch cubes

150 grams red pumpkin (*lal bhopla/kaddu*), peeled, seeded and cut into 1-inch cubes

½ small snake gourd, cut into 1-inch cubes

10-12 ladies' fingers, chopped

½ cup fresh corn kernels, blanched

5-6 green chillies, slit

salt to taste

½ cup chopped fresh coriander leaves

3 tablespoons oil

¾ cup grated fresh coconut

1 tablespoon pure *ghee*

1 teaspoon cumin seeds

- Place all the vegetables, the cooked corn, green chillies, salt, coriander leaves, oil, coconut and half a cup of water in a pressure cooker till the pressure is released three times (three whistles).

- Remove the lid when the pressure has reduced completely and simmer vegetables till extra water, if any, dries up. Heat the *ghee* in a small pan; sauté the cumin seeds and pour over the vegetables. Stir and serve hot.

Main Course - Vegetarian

PUMPKIN CURRY

250 grams unpeeled red pumpkin (*lal bhopla/kaddu*), diced
4 tablespoons grated fresh coconut
½ teaspoon mustard seeds
4 garlic cloves
2 tablespoons oil
7-8 curry leaves
1 medium onion, chopped
salt to taste
¼ teaspoon turmeric powder
4 green chillies, slit
1 cup coconut milk
1 teaspoon red chilli powder
1 tablespoon chopped fresh coriander leaves

- Grind the coconut, mustard seeds and garlic to a fine paste.

- Heat the oil in a pressure cooker; add the curry leaves. When they begin to change colour, add the onion and sauté till pink.

- Add the pumpkin, salt and turmeric powder and sauté for two or three minutes.

- Add the slit green chillies and coconut milk and bring to a boil. Seal the cooker with the lid and cook over medium heat till the pressure is released once (one whistle). The pumpkin should be completely cooked and tender.

- Remove the lid when the pressure has reduced completely. Add the ground paste and chilli powder and mix well. Simmer for three or four minutes.

- Garnish with coriander leaves and serve hot with steamed rice.

47

Main Course - Vegetarian

VEGETABLE STEW

2 medium carrots, cut into 1-inch pieces

¼ small cauliflower, separated into florets

¼ cup shelled green peas

1 medium zucchini, cut into 1-inch pieces

2 medium potatoes, cut into 1-inch pieces

1 inch ginger, sliced

3-4 cloves

8-10 black peppercorns

1 teaspoon cumin seeds

2 tablespoons oil

1 medium onion, sliced

1½ tablespoons refined flour (*maida*)

4½ cups Vegetable Stock (page 14)

salt to taste

1 celery stalk, cut into 1-inch pieces

3-4 black peppercorns, crushed

5 fresh spinach leaves (*palak*), shredded

2 loaves garlic bread, sliced

butter, as required

- Tie the ginger, cloves, peppercorns and cumin seeds in a piece of muslin to make a *bouquet garni*.

- Heat the oil in a pressure cooker; add the onion and sauté lightly. Add the refined flour and sauté for two minutes. Add the vegetable stock gradually, to prevent lumps from forming and bring the mixture to a boil.

- Add the *bouquet garni* to the boiling stock and season with salt. Add the potatoes.

- Seal the cooker with the lid and cook over medium heat till the pressure is released twice (two whistles.) Open the cooker when the pressure has reduced. Remove the *bouquet garni* and discard.

- Add the celery, carrots, cauliflower, green peas and zucchini. Seal the cooker with the lid and cook till the pressure is released once (one whistle). Remove from heat and leave to cool. Adjust salt and add the crushed peppercorns.

- Add the spinach and mix well. Cook for two minutes over low heat.

- Lightly toast the bread slices and spread with butter. Serve with the hot stew.

BHARLI VANGI

8-10 small brinjals (*vangi*)
1 lemon-sized ball tamarind
¾ cup grated fresh coconut
2 tablespoons chopped
fresh coriander leaves
4 tablespoons oil
2 medium onions, thinly sliced
¼ cup grated dried coconut
(*khopra*)
2 tablespoons sesame seeds (*til*)

¼ cup peanuts
½ teaspoon cumin seeds
1 teaspoon coriander seeds
2 teaspoons Goda Masala
salt to taste
¼ teaspoon turmeric powder
1½ teaspoons red chilli powder
½ teaspoon mustard seeds
6-8 curry leaves

- Slit the brinjals into four, lengthways keeping the stems intact. Soak in water.
- Soak the tamarind in half a cup of warm water for half an hour. Extract the pulp, strain and set aside.
- Reserve one tablespoon each of the grated coconut and coriander leaves for garnishing.

Main Course - Vegetarian

- Heat one tablespoon of oil in a pan; add the onions and sauté for a few minutes.
- Add the dried coconut, sesame seeds, peanuts, cumin seeds and coriander seeds and sauté over medium heat for two minutes, stirring continuously, till the dried coconut turns a light golden brown.
- Cool and grind the fried spice with a little water to a coarse paste. Combine the paste with the *goda masala*, salt, turmeric powder, chilli powder, remaining grated coconut and coriander leaves and tamarind pulp. Stuff the mixture into the brinjals.
- Heat the remaining oil in a pressure cooker; add the mustard seeds and when they beging to splutter, add the curry leaves.
- Place the stuffed brinjals in the pressure cooker and cook for two or three minutes. Gently turn the brinjals once or twice to cook evenly on all sides. Add half a cup of water and bring to a boil.
- Seal the pressure cooker with the lid and cook over medium heat till the pressure is released twice (two whistles). Remove the lid when the pressure has reduced completely and cook for one or two minutes. Serve hot, garnished with the reserved coriander leaves and grated coconut.

Note: *Goda Masala is a Maharashtrian blend of spices.*

Pressure Cooking

DAL GOSHT

¼ cup split Bengal gram (*chana dal*), soaked

⅛ cup split pigeon peas (*arhar dal/toovar dal*), soaked

⅛ cup split lentils (*masoor dal*), soaked

250 grams boneless mutton, cut into 1-inch cubes

2 tablespoons oil

½ teaspoon cumin seeds

2 green chillies, slit

¼ tablespoon ginger paste

½ tablespoon garlic paste

1 large onion, chopped

1 medium tomato, chopped

salt to taste

1 teaspoon red chilli powder

1 teaspoon coriander powder

1 teaspoon cumin powder

¼ teaspoon turmeric powder

¼ teaspoon *garam masala* powder

½ tablespoon lemon juice

2 tablespoons chopped fresh coriander leaves

- Heat the oil in a pressure cooker. Add the cumin seeds and green chillies and sauté till the cumin seeds begin to change colour. Add the ginger paste and garlic paste and sauté for half a minute.

- Add the onion and sauté till golden brown. Add the tomato and salt and continue to sauté for two more minutes.

- Add the chilli powder, coriander powder, cumin powder, turmeric powder and mutton and sauté for two minutes. Stir in the *garam masala* powder.

- Add one cup of water and bring to a boil. Seal the cooker with the lid and cook till the pressure is released twice (two whistles).

- When the pressure has reduced completely, add the soaked *dals* and four-and-a-half cups of water. Bring to a boil, cover the pressure cooker and cook under pressure till the pressure is released eight to ten times (eight to ten whistles).

- Once again allow the pressure to reduce. Remove the lid, stir and mash the *dals* lightly. Stir in the lemon juice and coriander leaves and simmer for five minutes. Serve hot.

54

BHATINDA MUTTON CURRY

800 grams mutton on the bone,
cut into 1-inch pieces
3 tablespoons oil
5-6 cloves
2 one-inch sticks cinnamon
3-4 green cardamoms
3 large onions, chopped
1 tablespoon ginger paste
1 tablespoon garlic paste

1 tablespoon red chilli powder
1 tablespoon coriander powder
1 teaspoon turmeric powder
4 medium potatoes, halved
salt to taste
1 cup yogurt, whisked
1 teaspoon *garam masala* powder
2 tablespoons chopped fresh
coriander leaves

- Heat the oil in a pressure cooker; add the cloves, cinnamon, cardamoms and onions and sauté till the onions turn golden brown.

- Add the ginger paste, garlic paste, chilli powder, coriander powder and turmeric powder and sauté for two minutes.

Pressure Cooking

- Add the mutton and potatoes and sauté for three or four minutes. Add two cups of water and salt and bring to a boil. Seal the cooker with the lid and cook over medium heat till the pressure is released six times (six whistles).

- Remove the lid when the pressure has reduced completely; stir in the yogurt and *garam masala* powder and simmer for five minutes.

- Serve hot, garnished with coriander leaves.

Main Course - Non-Vegetarian

STEAMED TANDOORI POMFRET

2 (225 grams each) pomfrets
salt to taste
2 tablespoons lemon juice
2 teaspoons ginger paste
2 teaspoons garlic paste
½ teaspoon carom seeds (*ajwain*)

½ cup yogurt
2 tablespoons gram flour (*besan*)
½ teaspoon turmeric powder
1 teaspoon *garam masala* powder
2 teaspoons butter or oil
1 lemon, cut into wedges

- Make slits on both sides of the pomfrets and rub in the salt and lemon juice. Set aside for twenty minutes.

- Mix together all the other ingredients except the butter or oil. Spread the marinade over the fish and leave to stand for about one hour in a refrigerator.

- Place the fish on a plate and place in a pressure cooker. Do not add any water. Remove the gasket from the lid, cover the cooker with the lid and cook for ten to fifteen minutes, basting with butter in between.

- Serve hot with lemon wedges.

Pressure Cooking

MALVANI MUTTON

800 grams mutton on the bone, cut
into 1-inch cubes
5 tablespoons oil
4 medium onions, finely sliced
1½ tablespoons ginger paste
1½ tablespoons garlic paste
salt to taste
¾ teaspoon turmeric powder
2 tablespoons chopped fresh
coriander leaves

Masala Paste
12 dried red chillies
3 teaspoons coriander seeds
6-8 cloves
7-8 black peppercorns
¾ teaspoon cumin seeds
¾ teaspoon caraway seeds
(*shahi jeera*)
6 green cardamoms
4 black cardamoms
¾ cup grated dried coconut
(*khopra*)
1½ teaspoons poppy seeds
(*khuskhus*)

Main Course - Non-Vegetarian

- Dry-roast the red chillies, coriander seeds, cloves, peppercorns, cumin seeds, caraway seeds, green cardamoms, black cardamoms, dried coconut and poppy seeds, separately, on a hot *tawa* till fragrant.

- Grind all the roasted ingredients together with a little water to a fine paste.

- Heat the oil in a pressure cooker; add the onions and sauté till light golden brown.

- Add the ginger paste and garlic paste and sauté for thirty seconds.

- Add the mutton and sauté for three or four minutes; add four cups of water and salt to taste. Seal the cooker with the lid and cook over medium heat till the pressure is released six times (six whistles).

- Remove the lid when the pressure has completely reduced. Add the ground *masala* and turmeric powder and mix well. If the gravy is too thick, add half a cup of water and simmer for two or three minutes.

- Serve hot, garnished with coriander leaves.

KOLHAPURI CHICKEN

1 whole (1 kilogram) chicken, cut into 12 pieces
5 tablespoons oil
3-4 dried red chillies
3 medium onions, chopped
2 teaspoons ginger paste
2 teaspoons garlic paste
¼ teaspoon turmeric powder
a pinch of grated nutmeg
1 teaspoon Kolhapuri Dry Chutney
salt to taste
2 tablespoons chopped fresh coriander leaves

Masala Paste
1 tablespoon sesame seeds (*til*)
2 tablespoons poppy seeds (*khuskhus*)
6-8 black peppercorns
1 teaspoon caraway seeds (*shahi jeera*)
1 tablespoon cumin seeds
1 inch cinnamon
3-4 green cardamoms
1 black cardamom
4-5 cloves
1 blade of mace (*javitri*)
¼ dried coconut, grated
8-10 Bedgi red chillies

Main Course - Non-Vegetarian

- For the masala paste, dry-roast the sesame seeds, poppy seeds, peppercorns, caraway seeds, cumin seeds, cinnamon, green cardamoms, black cardamom, cloves, mace, dried coconut and Bedgi chillies separately. Cool and grind with a little water to a fine paste.

- Heat the oil in a pressure cooker; add the red chillies, sauté for a few seconds, remove from heat and reserve for garnishing. Add the onions to the same oil and sauté till golden brown.

- Add the ginger paste and garlic paste and cook over medium heat for a few seconds.

- Stir in the ground paste and cook for three or four minutes over medium heat, stirring frequently.

- Add the chicken, mix well and cook over high heat, stirring continuously, for two or three minutes.

- Add half a cup of water and continue cooking over medium heat for three or four minutes, stirring frequently.

- Add the turmeric powder, grated nutmeg, Kolhapuri dry chutney and salt. Seal the cooker with the lid and cook till the pressure is released twice (two whistles). Remove the lid when the pressure has reduced. The *masala* should be quite thick and dry.

- Serve hot, garnished with coriander leaves and fried chillies.

Kolhapuri Dry Chutney

Kolhapuri Dry Chutney is a spicy mixture of dried coconut, red chillies and assorted spices. It is available in specialty grocery stores and supermarkets.

DAHI KA GOSHT

800 grams boneless mutton, cubed
1½ cups yogurt
3 tablespoons oil
2 medium onions, sliced
2 teaspoons ginger paste
2 teaspoons garlic paste
5 green chillies, minced
salt to taste

2 bay leaves
1 teaspoon coriander powder
1 teaspoon cumin powder
½ teaspoon mace-cardamom powder
2 tablespoons chopped fresh coriander leaves

- Heat one tablespoon of oil in a *kadai* and sauté the onions till brown. Grind the onions to a fine paste.

- Marinate the mutton in a mixture of the yogurt, ginger paste, garlic paste, minced green chillies and salt for one hour, preferably in a refrigerator.

Main Course - Non-Vegetarian

- Heat the remaining oil in a pressure cooker and add the bay leaves.

- Add the marinated mutton and cook till the gravy comes to a boil. Stir in the coriander powder, cumin powder, browned onion paste and half a cup of water.

- Seal the cooker with the lid and cook till the pressure is released six times (six whistles). Remove the lid when the pressure has reduced completely and sprinkle the mace-cardamom powder over the mutton.

- Serve hot, garnished with chopped coriander leaves.

CHICKEN CAFREAL

1 whole (1 kilogram) chicken, cut into 8 pieces
3 tablespoons oil + for deep-frying
2 medium onions, finely sliced
1 tablespoon coriander seeds
1 teaspoon cumin seeds
6 cloves
8 green cardamoms
8 black peppercorns
1 inch cinnamon
1 inch ginger, roughly chopped
4-5 garlic cloves, roughly chopped
6 green chillies, roughly chopped
salt to taste
3 tablespoons vinegar

- Make deep incisions in the chicken pieces with a sharp knife.

- Heat the oil in a *kadai* and deep-fry the onions till crisp and golden brown. Drain on absorbent paper and reserve for garnishing.

- Dry-roast the coriander seeds, cumin seeds, cloves, cardamoms, peppercorns and cinnamon. Grind the roasted spices, ginger, garlic and green chillies with a little water to a fine paste. Add salt to taste

Main Course - Non-Vegetarian

- Rub the paste over the chicken and marinate for two or three hours, in a regfigerator.

- Heat three tablespoons of oil in a pressure cooker. Add the marinated chicken and sauté over medium heat for one minute. Add one-fourth cup of warm water, seal the cooker with the lid and cook over medium heat till the pressure is released once or twice (one or two whistles).

- Remove the lid when the pressure has reduced completely and stir in the vinegar. Cook for one or two minutes.

- Serve hot, garnished with fried onions.

Chef's Tip: *I know of a Goan restaurant, which adds a little fresh coriander to the paste and it tastes delicious.*

BHUNA KUKDA

1 whole (1 kilogram) chicken, cut
into 8 pieces
12 garlic cloves
20 dried red chillies, soaked
4-5 cloves
4 green cardamoms
2 inches cinnamon

1 teaspoon turmeric powder
salt to taste
2 tablespoons mustard oil
1 teaspoon cumin seeds
½ cup yogurt, whisked
½ cup chopped fresh coriander
leaves

- Grind together the garlic, red chillies, cloves, cardamoms, cinnamon and turmeric powder to a fine paste.

- Rub the paste and salt over the chicken and leave to marinate for two hours in a refrigerator.

- Heat the oil in a pressure cooker; add the cumin seeds and when they begin to change colour, add the marinated chicken and sauté over high heat.

Main Course - Non-Vegetarian

- When all the moisture has evaporated, add the yogurt with half a cup of water. Seal the cooker with the lid and cook till the pressure is released twice (two whistles).

- Remove the lid when the pressure has reduced completely. Stir-fry till the *masala* coats the chicken.

- Serve hot, sprinkled with coriander leaves.

METHI CHICKEN

1 whole (800 grams) chicken, cut into 8 pieces

½ bunch (125 grams) fresh fenugreek leaves (*methi*), chopped

4 tablespoons oil

1 cup yogurt, whisked

salt to taste

4 inches ginger

5 green cardamoms

1 black cardamom

5 cloves

1 inch cinnamon

1 bay leaf

1-2 blades of mace (*javitri*)

2 large onions, chopped

20 garlic cloves, chopped

3 green chillies, seeded and chopped

½ teaspoon turmeric powder

1 teaspoon coriander powder

1 teaspoon red chilli powder

2 medium tomatoes, chopped

1 tablespoon dried fenugreek leaves (*kasoori methi*), roasted and crushed

3 tablespoons chopped fresh coriander leaves

Pressure Cooking

- Mix together the yogurt and salt in a large bowl. Mix in the chicken and leave to marinate for about half an hour. Chop half the ginger and cut the rest into thin strips.

- Heat the oil in a pressure cooker. Add the green and black cardamom, cloves, cinnamon, bay leaf and mace and sauté for one minute. Add the onions and sauté till golden brown. Add the garlic, chopped ginger and green chillies and sauté for two minutes.

- Stir in the turmeric powder, coriander powder, chilli powder and one-fourth cup of water. Add the tomatoes and cook till soft and pulpy.

- Add the marinated chicken and fenugreek leaves and mix well. Seal the cooker with the lid and cook over medium heat till the pressure is released twice (two whistles).

- Remove the lid when the pressure has reduced completely.

- Sprinkle *kasoori methi*, ginger strips and coriander leaves over the chicken. Cover and leave to stand for about five minutes before serving.

Main Course - Non-Vegetarian

MASALA PRAWNS

40 (500 grams) medium prawns, peeled and deveined
2 tablespoons oil
1 teaspoon cumin seeds
2 medium onions, chopped
1 inch ginger, chopped
2 green chillies, chopped
1 teaspoon red chilli powder
¼ cup chopped fresh coriander leaves
2 medium tomatoes, chopped
4 tablespoons tomato purée
salt to taste
½ teaspoon sugar
2 teaspoons lemon juice
½ teaspoon *garam masala* powder

- Heat the oil in a pressure cooker; add the cumin seeds and sauté till they begin to change colour. Add the onions and sauté till light brown. Add the ginger and green chillies.

- Add the chilli powder, half the coriander leaves, the tomatoes, tomato purée, salt, sugar and lemon juice, and cook till the oil separates.

Pressure Cooking

- Add the prawns with half a cup of water, seal the cooker with the lid and cook over medium heat till the pressure is released once (one whistle).

- Remove the lid when the pressure has reduced completely and sprinkle *garam masala* powder over the prawns.

- Serve hot, garnished with the remaining coriander leaves.

Main Course - Non-Vegetarian

LANGAR KI DAL

1 cup whole black gram (*sabut urad*), soaked overnight
1 inch ginger, chopped
8 garlic cloves, chopped
1 green chilli, slit
salt to taste
¼ teaspoon turmeric powder
4 tablespoons *ghee*
1 teaspoon cumin seeds
4 medium onions, chopped
2 teaspoons *garam masala* powder

- Soak the *dal* overnight, or for at least six hours. Drain and cook under pressure with the ginger, garlic, green chilli, salt, turmeric powder, one tablespoon *ghee* and three cups of water till the pressure is released six times (six whistles).

- Heat the remaining *ghee* in a pan; add the cumin seeds and sauté till they begin to change colour. Add the onions and sauté till golden brown.

- Stir in the cooked *dal*. Add one cup of water if the mixture is too thick. Add the *garam masala* powder and simmer for two or three minutes. Serve hot.

Pressure Cooking

SHAHI PRAWN PULAO

300 grams medium prawns, peeled
and deveined
1½ cups Basmati rice, soaked
4 tablespoons oil
3 large onions, sliced
2 teaspoons ginger-garlic paste
2 medium tomatoes, chopped
2 green chillies, slit

2 teaspoons red chilli powder
½ teaspoon turmeric powder
salt to taste
½ cup coconut milk
¼ cup yogurt
1 teaspoon *garam masala* powder
1 tablespoon chopped fresh
coriander leaves

- Heat the oil in a pressure cooker. Add the onions and sauté till pale gold. Add the ginger-garlic paste and sauté for one minute.

- Add the tomatoes and continue to sauté till the tomatoes soften.

- Add the green chillies and chilli powder and sauté till the oil begins to separate.

- Add the turmeric powder, prawns and salt. Sauté for two minutes and add the coconut milk and yogurt. Stir in the *garam masala* powder and simmer for two minutes over low heat.

- Add the drained rice and stir lightly. Add two cups of water and bring to a boil. Seal the cooker with the lid and cook over medium heat till the pressure is released twice (two whistles).

- Open the lid when the pressure has reduced completely, garnish with coriander leaves and serve hot.

Dals and Cereals

CHANE JAISELMER KE

½ cup Bengal gram (*kale chane*)
1½ cups yogurt
4 teaspoons gram flour (*besan*)
¼ teaspoon turmeric powder
salt to taste
1 teaspoon red chilli powder
2 teaspoons coriander powder

1 teaspoon *garam masala* powder
3-4 green chillies, chopped
4 tablespoons pure *ghee*
a pinch of asafoetida (*hing*)
1 teaspoon cumin seeds
2 tablespoons chopped fresh
   coriander leaves

- Soak the *kale chane* overnight in four cups of water. Drain.

- Add four cups of water and cook the *chane* till the pressure is released four times (four whistles). Drain and reserve the liquid. Empty the *chane* into a bowl and mash lightly.

- In a bowl, mix together the yogurt, gram flour, turmeric powder, salt, chilli powder, coriander powder and *garam masala* powder and mix till smooth. Stir in the green chillies and one cup of the reserved liquid.

Pressure Cooking

- Heat the *ghee* in a pan; add the asafoetida and cumin seeds. When they begin to change colour, stir in the yogurt mixture. Add the *chane*, salt and some more of the reserved liquid. Bring to a boil and cook for five minutes.

- Garnish with coriander leaves and serve hot.

MUTTON KHICHDA

½ kilogram boneless mutton, cut into ½-inch cubes

½ cup broken wheat (*lapsi/dalia*)

1 tablespoon split black gram (*dhuli urad dal*)

1 tablespoon split Bengal gram (*chana dal*)

1 tablespoon split green gram (*dhuli moong dal*)

1 cup yogurt

salt to taste

4 large onions, thinly sliced

oil for deep-frying

1 tablespoon green chilli paste

1 tablespoon ginger-garlic paste

1 teaspoon caraway seeds (*shahi jeera*)

1 teaspoon black peppercorns

½ teaspoon turmeric powder

6 cups Mutton Stock (page 95)

1 tablespoon chopped fresh mint leaves

1 teaspoon *garam masala* powder

¼ cup pure *ghee*

½ cup milk

a few sprigs of fresh mint leaves

3-4 lemon wedges

Pressure Cooking

- Soak the broken wheat for three or four hours in two cups of water. Soak the *dhuli urad dal*, *chana dal* and *moong dal* in one cup of water.

- Marinate the mutton with the yogurt and salt for one hour, preferably in a refrigerator.

- Heat the oil in a *kadai* and deep-fry the onion slices till golden. Drain on absorbent paper.

- Place the soaked broken wheat, *urad dal*, *chana dal* and *moong dal* in a pressure cooker. Add the marinated mutton, green chilli paste, ginger-garlic paste, *shahi jeera*, peppercorns and turmeric powder and mix.

- Stir in the mutton stock. Add the salt, mint leaves, *garam masala* powder and half the fried onions. Seal the cooker with the lid and cook for thirty to forty minutes.

- Remove the lid when the pressure is reduced completely and remove the mutton with a slotted spoon. Purée the rest of the mixture in a blender. Put the mutton back into the mixture.

- Heat the *ghee* in a pan. Pour the *khichda* into it and bring to a boil. Lower heat and simmer for ten minutes. Adjust the consistency by adding milk.

- Serve, garnished with the remaining fried onions, the sprigs of mint and lemon wedges.

Dals and Cereals

BROWN RICE VEGETABLE PILAF

2 cups Basmati brown rice
½ cup green peas, shelled
2 medium carrots, diced
10-12 French beans, chopped
¼ medium cauliflower, separated into florets
6-7 fresh medium button mushrooms, halved
2 tablespoons oil
1 bay leaf

2-3 cloves
1 teaspoon cumin seeds
2 one-inch sticks cinnamon
2 medium onions, sliced
¼ teaspoon turmeric powder
Salt to taste
4 green chillies, slit
½ teaspoon *garam masala* powder
100 grams silken tofu (bean curd), cut into ½-inch cubes

- Soak the brown rice in four or five cups of water for one hour. Drain and set aside.

- Heat the oil in a pressure cooker. Add the bay leaf, cloves, cumin seeds and cinnamon. When they begin to change colour add the onions and sauté till light brown.

Pressure Cooking

- Add the drained rice, turmeric powder and salt and sauté for one or two minutes. Add five cups of water and bring to a boil. Seal the cooker with the lid and cook over a medium heat till the pressure is released four times (four whistles). Remove the lid when the pressure reduces completely.

- Add the green peas, carrots, French beans, cauliflower, mushrooms, green chillies and *garam masala* powder. Stir and cover once more with the lid. Pressure-cook over a medium heat till the pressure is released twice (two whistles).

- Serve hot, garnished with the tofu.

SURAN KI KHICHDI

250 grams *suran*, cut into ½-inch cubes

1 cup rice

½ cup split green gram (*dhuli moong dal*)

2 tablespoons pure *ghee*

1 teaspoon cumin seeds

4 cloves

1 inch cinnamon

1 medium carrot, cut into ½-inch cubes

4-5 French beans, cut into ½-inch pieces

2 medium tomatoes, chopped

½ teaspoon turmeric powder

1 teaspoon red chilli powder

salt to taste

- Soak the rice and *moong dal* together in three cups of water for one hour. Drain and set aside.

- Heat the *ghee* in a pressure cooker; add the cumin seeds, cloves and cinnamon. When the spices begin to change colour, add the *suran*, carrot and French beans. Sauté for three or four minutes.

Pressure Cooking

- Add the tomatoes, turmeric powder, chilli powder and salt and continue to sauté for two or three minutes.

- Add the rice, *dal* and three cups of water. Bring to a boil and seal the cooker with the lid. Cook over medium heat till the pressure is released three times (three whistles). Remove the lid when the pressure has reduced completely.

- Serve hot.

Dals and Cereals

PALAKWALI DAL

15-20 fresh spinach leaves (*palak*), roughly shredded

¾ cup split green gram (*dhuli moong dal*)

salt to taste

1 teaspoon turmeric powder

2 tablespoons oil

a pinch of asafoetida (*hing*)

1 teaspoon cumin seeds

2 medium onions, chopped

2 green chillies, seeded and chopped

1 inch ginger, chopped

6-8 garlic cloves, chopped

1 teaspoon lemon juice

- Cook the *moong dal* with salt, turmeric powder and five cups of water in a pressure cooker till the pressure is released twice (two whistles).

- Heat the oil in a *kadai*; add the asafoetida and cumin seeds. When the cumin seeds begin to change colour, add the onions and green chillies. Cook till the onions are soft and translucent.

- Add the ginger and garlic and cook for half a minute. Add the *dal*, bring to a boil, and stir in the spinach and lemon juice. Simmer for two minutes and serve hot.

Pressure Cooking

GEHUN KI KHICHDI

2 cups broken wheat (*lapsi/dalia*)
4 tablespoons oil
1 teaspoon cumin seeds
a pinch of asafoetida (*hing*)
1 medium carrot, cut into
½-inch pieces
10 French beans, cut into
½-inch pieces

1 medium potato, cut into
½ inch pieces
2 medium tomatoes, chopped
salt to taste
2 tablespoons chopped fresh
coriander leaves

- Soak the broken wheat in three cups of water for half an hour. Drain and set aside.

- Heat the oil in a pressure cooker; add the cumin seeds and when they begin to change colour add the asafoetida, carrot, French beans, potato and tomatoes. Sauté for a while.

Pressure Cooking

- Add the drained wheat and sauté for three or four minutes.
- Add five cups of water and salt, Seal the cooker with the lid and cook over medium heat till the pressure is released twice (two whistles). Lower the heat and cook for another five minutes.
- Remove the lid when the pressure has reduced completely.
- Serve, garnished with coriander leaves.

HERBED RICE WITH MUSHROOMS

1½ cups brown rice
6-7 medium fresh button
    mushrooms, halved
2 tablespoons olive oil
2 medium onions, chopped

2-3 garlic cloves, chopped
1 inch celery stalk, chopped
salt to taste
1 teaspoon dried oregano

- Soak the brown rice in four or five cups of water for one hour. Drain.
- Heat the oil in a pressure cooker. Add the onions, garlic and celery and sauté till translucent.
- Add the drained rice and salt and sauté for one or two minutes. Add three and three-quarter cups of water and bring to a boil.
- Stir in the mushrooms and bring to a boil again. Seal the cooker with the lid and cook till the pressure is released three times (three whistles).
- Remove the lid once the pressure has reduced. Add the dried oregano and mix. Serve hot.

Pressure Cooking

CHICKEN PULAO

1½ cups Basmati rice, soaked
600 grams boneless chicken,
cut into 1½-inch pieces
½ cup yogurt
2 tablespoons ginger paste
2 tablespoons garlic paste
salt to taste
4 tablespoons oil
1 teaspoon cumin seeds

6-8 cloves
2 inches cinnamon
6-8 green cardamoms
2 bay leaves
2 medium onions, sliced
3 medium tomatoes, chopped
1 teaspoon red chilli powder
3 cups Chicken Stock (see below)

- Marinate the chicken in a mixture of the yogurt, ginger paste, garlic paste and salt for one hour, preferably in a refrigerator.
- Heat the oil in a pressure cooker; add the cumin seeds and sauté for ten seconds. Add the cloves, cinnamon, cardamoms and bay leaves. Sauté again for about ten seconds.

Pressure Cooking

- Add the onions and sauté till golden brown. Add the tomatoes and cook over high heat for three minutes, stirring continuously. Add the chilli powder and stir to mix. Add the chicken with the marinade and sauté for two or three minutes. Pour in the chicken stock and bring to a boil.

- Stir in the rice and bring to a boil again. Seal the cooker with the lid and cook over medium heat till the pressure releases twice (two whistles).

- Remove the lid when the pressure has reduced completely and stir lightly to separate the rice grains.

- Serve with *raita* and *kachumber*.

Mutton/Chicken Stock

Wash and clean 200 grams of chicken/mutton bones, removing any excess fat. Boil in water to cover for five minutes. Drain and discard the liquid. Boil blanched bones, 1 chopped onion, 1 carrot, cut into large pieces, 1 stalk of celery and 2-3 stalks of parsley, both cut into 2-3 inch pieces, 6-7 black peppercorns and 1 bay leaf in a deep pan with 10 cups of water. Simmer for at least one hour, removing any scum which rises to the top. Strain and use as required.

Dals and Cereals

VEGETABLE BIRYANI

1½ cups Basmati rice, soaked

4 medium carrots, cut into ½-inch pieces

10-12 cauliflower florets

15 French beans, cut into ½-inch pieces

1 cup shelled green peas

a few saffron threads

¼ cup warm milk

salt to taste

2 green cardamoms

1 black cardamom

4 cloves

½ inch cinnamon

1 bay leaf

oil for deep-frying

4 large onions, sliced

1½ cups yogurt

1½ tablespoons ginger-garlic paste

4-5 green chillies, chopped

1 tablespoon coriander powder

1 teaspoon turmeric powder

1 tablespoon red chilli powder

¾ teaspoon *garam masala* powder

2 tablespoons chopped fresh coriander leaves

2 tablespoons chopped fresh mint leaves

a few drops of *kewra* essence (optional)

2 inches ginger, cut into thin strips

Pressure Cooking

- Soak the saffron in the warm milk.
- Drain and boil the rice in four cups of boiling salted water with green and black cardamoms, cloves, cinnamon and bay leaf, until three-fourth done. Drain excess water.
- Heat the oil in a *kadai* and deep-fry the onions till golden. Drain on absorbent paper.
- Blanch all the vegetables separately. Drain and refresh in cold water.
- In a bowl, mix the vegetables with the yogurt, ginger-garlic paste, green chillies, coriander powder, turmeric powder, chilli powder, half the *garam masala* powder, salt and half the browned onions. Transfer the mixture to a pressure cooker.
- Spread the rice over the vegetables. Sprinkle the saffron-flavoured milk, coriander leaves, mint leaves, *kewra* essence, ginger strips, remaining *garam masala* powder and remaining browned onions over the rice.
- Seal the cooker with the lid and cook over medium heat, without the weight, till the rice and vegetables are done. This may take around fifteen to twenty minutes.
- Serve hot with a *raita* of your choice.

Dals and Cereals

CHOCOLATE MODAK

1 cup rice flour
a pinch of salt
1 teaspoon oil

Stuffing
¼ cup chocolate syrup
½ cup grated chocolate
¾ cup desiccated coconut

- Boil one cup of water in a pan with salt and oil.
- Pour the rice flour in a steady stream, stirring continuously, to prevent lumps from forming.
- Seal the cooker with the lid and cook till steam begins to escape. Remove the lid and sprinkle water over the dough , seal the cooker with the lid and cook till steam begins to escape again. Mix well and remove the dough to a plate.
- Grease your palms with some oil and knead the dough till smooth. Divide the dough into eight equal portions.
- For the stuffing, mix together the coconut, chocolate syrup and grated chocolate and divide into eight equal portions.

Pressure Cooking

- Grease your palms again, and spread one portion of the dough into a disc, thinning the edges with your finger tips.
- Place one portion of the coconut mixture in the centre, gather the dough together in tiny pleats and press lightly to form a cone at the top.
- Place the *modaks* on a perforated plate and steam in a pressure cooker, with the lid on but without the weight, for ten to twelve minutes.
- Serve hot.

99

GAJAR HALWA

7 medium carrots, grated
2 tablespoons pure *ghee*
½ cup milk
7 tablespoons sugar
½ cup grated *khoya/mawa*

¼ teaspoon green cardamom powder
1 tablespoon raisins (*kishmish*)
5-6 cashew nuts, chopped
5-6 almonds, blanched, chopped

- Heat the *ghee* in a pressure cooker; add the carrots and sauté for five minutes. Add the milk and sugar, seal the cooker with the lid and cook till the pressure releases four times (four whistles).

- Remove the lid when the pressure has reduced completely and stir in the *khoya*.

- Cook for two or three minutes, stirring continuously. Stir in the cardamom powder. Continue to cook till the excess liquid evaporates.

- Add the raisins, cashew nuts and almonds and continue to cook for two more minutes. Serve hot or at room temperature.

Pressure Cooking

DOODHI HALWA

600 grams bottle gourd
(*lauki/doodhi*)
2 tablespoons *ghee*
7 tablespoons sugar
¼ cup grated *khoya/mawa*

¼ teaspoon green cardamom
powder
1 tablespoon raisins (*kishmish*)
5-6 cashew nuts, chopped
5-6 almonds, blanched, slivered

- Peel and grate the *doodhi*.

- Heat the *ghee* in a pressure cooker. Add the *doodhi* and sauté for five minutes. Add the sugar, seal the cooker with the lid and cook over medium heat till the pressure is released three times (three whistles).

- Remove the lid when the pressure has reduced completely and add the *khoya* and cardamom powder. Cook, stirring continuously, for two or three minutes, or till the excess liquid evaporates.

- Add the raisins, cashew nuts and almonds and continue to cook for two more minutes. Serve hot or at room temperature.

Desserts

KHARVAS

¾ litre colostrum (*cheek*) ¾ teaspoon green cardamom powder
¾ litre milk a pinch of nutmeg powder
1¼ cups sugar a few saffron threads

- Mix all the ingredients well.
- Heat some water in a pressure cooker.

- Pour the mixture into a deep container and steam in the pressure cooker for ten minutes over medium heat. Lower heat and continue to steam for fifteen minutes longer.
- Remove the container from the cooker and set aside to cool. Chill in a refrigerator for a couple of hours.
- Cut into cubes and serve.

Note:

- *Colostrum is the first milk produced by the cow after it has given birth to a calf.*

- *Use equal quantities of milk and colostrum to prepare Kharvas if the colostrum used is from the first day after birth.*

- *Use half the quantity of milk to that of colostrum to prepare Kharvas if colostrum used is from the second day.*